PResident, long Must Wait for LIBeRty?

—INez MilHOLLAND

written by

Kirsten Gillibrand

BOLD & BRAVE

Ten Heroes who won Women the Right to Vote

art by

Maira Kalman

Alfred A. Knopf
New York

THIS IS A BORZOI BOOK PUBLISHED BY ALFRED A. KNOPF

Text copyright © 2018 by Kirsten Gillibrand
Jacket art and interior illustrations copyright © 2018 by Maira Kalman

All rights reserved. Published in the United States by Alfred A. Knopf, an imprint of
Random House Children's Books, a division of Penguin Random House LLC, New York.

Knopf, Borzoi Books, and the colophon are registered trademarks of Penguin Random House LLC.

Visit us on the Web! rhcbooks.com

Educators and librarians, for a variety of teaching tools, visit us at RHTeachersLibrarians.com

Library of Congress Cataloging-in-Publication Data is available upon request.
ISBN 978-0-525-57901-4 (trade) — ISBN 978-0-525-57902-1 (lib. bdg.) —
ISBN 978-0-525-57903-8 (ebook)

The text of this book is set in
15-point Filosofia.
The paintings were created using
gouache on paper.
Book design by Nicole de las Heras

Random House Children's Books
supports the First Amendment and
celebrates the right to read.

MANUFACTURED IN CHINA
November 2018
10 9 8 7 6 5 4 3 2 1

First Edition

To my mother,
who dared me to be different
—K.G.

To my beloved children
and their children
and their children
and
—M.K.

WOMEN!
USE
YOUR
VOTE

W_HEN I WAS A LITTLE GIRL, after church on Sundays, I would visit my great-grandmother Mimi. She told me about a time when women like her left their homes and worked in factories, making equipment to help American soldiers win the war. Mimi taught me to be bold and to believe there was nothing I couldn't do.

Mimi's oldest daughter was my grandmother Polly. She liked to roller-skate down the long marble hallways of the New York State Capitol, where she worked. When I was about ten, Grandma took me to a big room where ladies stuffed envelopes with letters urging people to vote. I thought, I want to be just like them someday! Grandma taught me to fight for what I believe in.

Grandma's oldest daughter was my mom, Penny. She always did what she set her mind to. She was a sportswriter for her student newspaper, even though girls were not allowed in the press boxes. She went on to law school and was one of only three women in her class. As a mom, she also earned her black belt in karate, something few women at the time aspired to. My mother taught me you need to be brave to forge a new path.

Who taught my mom and her mom and *her* mom to be bold and brave so they could teach me and you? I can tell you who. The women who came before them—women who faced unimaginable challenges.

Summer with my family

When my grandmother was born, women didn't have the right to vote. That meant they didn't have the power to elect the people who establish our country's rules and laws. Less than a century later, I became a United States senator, which means I help make those laws. Here are ten women who paved the way. They were called suffragists—not because they suffered, although they most certainly did, but because *suffrage* means "the right to vote." They fought so women could be heard.

Elizabeth Cady Stanton

1815–1902

Dare
to BE
DiFFERent

In 1848, Elizabeth Cady Stanton was a young mother when she and her friends decided to hold a big meeting about women's rights. They believed something uncommon at the time—that "all men *and women* are created equal"—and wanted laws to guarantee it. They especially wanted *the right to vote.* The three hundred women and men who attended this convention near Elizabeth's home in Seneca Falls, New York, became some of the earliest American suffragists.

People made fun of the suffragists, but Elizabeth didn't let that stop her. She was fearless. As a young girl, she rode horses, learned Greek, and played chess, all of which were typically just for boys. She once said, "The best protection any woman can have . . . is courage." This first convention, in July 1848, was only the beginning of her fifty-year effort to win voting rights for women. But she was not alone in her journey.

Susan _____ _____tionist, which means she opposed
slave_____ _____ convinced Susan to fight for women's
voting _____ _____y were a team. Some people said that
Eliza_____ _____lts" and Susan "fired them."

S_____ _____ by train and horse-drawn coach to rally
sup_____ _____ women, often wearing her favorite red silk
sh_____ _____e speak in school houses, barns, sawmills,
_____ _____ seats and lanterns hung around for lights, but
_____ _____es to hear us." Today, twenty miles may not
_____ ____rs, it could take all day—or longer—to travel that

_____d to vote for president and was arrested! She spoke
_____rs—until she died, almost fifteen years before women
_____ers carried the torch, and the amendment that finally
_____he right to vote—the Nineteenth Amendment—is also
_____ B. Anthony Amendment.

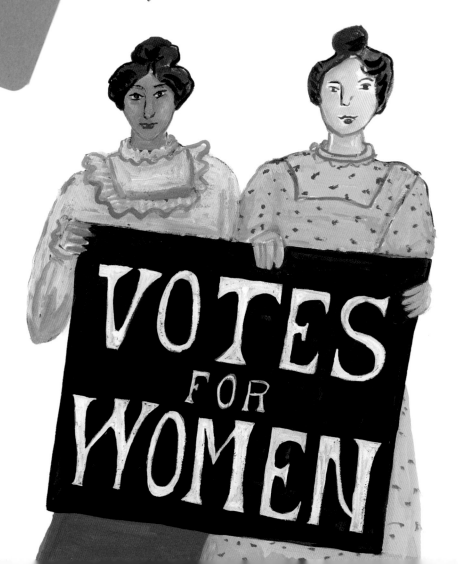

Sojourner Truth's given name was Isabella Bomefree. She was born into slavery in Ulster County, New York. She left her owner in 1826—the year before enslaved people were freed in her state. Years later, she changed her name. *Sojourner* means "someone who travels from place to place," and truth was at the center of her faith. She once said, "I will shake every place I go to," and she did exactly that.

Sojourner was one of the first African American women to successfully stand up for herself in court. Her young son was still enslaved, and

she sued to free him and won. Sojourner fought to end slavery and traveled the country pressing for equality for all. She worked with some of the most important thinkers of the day, such as abolitionist Frederick Douglass and President Abraham Lincoln. In 1851, she spoke at the Women's Rights Convention in Akron, Ohio, and in 1867 at the American Equal Rights Association meeting in New York. Sojourner asserted that all people deserved the

right to vote—no matter the color of their skin or if they were male or female. Sojourner lived to bring justice to others, proclaiming that "the truth is powerful and will prevail."

HaRRiet
TUBMAN

c. 1822-1913

BE
STRONG
and
COURAGEOUS

Harriet Tubman was born into slavery in Dorchester County, Maryland, and had a very hard life. But her faith and her family taught her that she was special, strong, and brave. In 1849, Harriet escaped from slavery, then spent years helping her family and others escape. She wrote a letter to a friend explaining why: "I have heard their groans and sighs, and seen their tears, and I would give every drop of blood in my veins to free them." She was a "conductor" on the Underground Railroad, a network of those who helped bring enslaved people to freedom. She ran *toward* danger, not away from it. Harriet was so courageous and so certain about what to do that people often called her General Tubman.

During the Civil War, Harriet served as a nurse, an armed scout, and a spy. After the war, she turned her efforts to gaining suffrage for all women, and was especially interested in the rights of African American women. In 1898, Harriet gave speeches for women's rights in New York City, Boston, and Washington, D.C. She continued to help people throughout her life. Today, designers at the U.S. Mint, which makes our money, are considering a new twenty-dollar bill bearing her image to honor her bravery and conviction.

JOVITA IDÁR

1885-1946

Fight
FOR
FAIRNESS

Jovita Idár was born in Laredo, Texas. Her father published a Spanish-language newspaper. Like him, Jovita loved to read and write—and to speak out. She became a teacher, a civil rights activist, a journalist, and—just like her dad—a newspaper publisher. She focused on the violence against and mistreatment of Mexican Americans and the importance of women's rights, including the right to vote.

In her first teaching job, Jovita found herself without books, pencils, or paper for the children. Many had no food, and sometimes the school had no heat in the winter. Jovita vowed to change that, and she did. In 1911, she helped found, and became the first president of, the League of Mexican Women, which focused on education and women's rights. She later started a free kindergarten, which provided school supplies, food, and clothing for the children. Jovita believed education was vital: "Educate a woman and you educate a family."

WOMEN UNITE

ALICE PAUL
1885-1977

SHAKE Things UP

lice Paul grew up in Mount Laurel, New Jersey. Later, she was a
student in England, where she saw women fighting for their
right to vote by using tactics that were shocking for the early 1900s—
protesting with signs, marching with banners, and even breaking
windows. Alice joined in their fight. Although she was arrested and
imprisoned, Alice believed American women needed to use these same
methods. Once home, Alice helped to organize the first national parade
for women's suffrage in Washington, D.C., on March 3, 1913. She chose
the day before the inauguration of the new president, Woodrow Wilson,
to pressure him and Congress to vote for national women's suffrage.

During the parade, five thousand women marched in elegant
white clothes, rode horses, and drove floats and cars. They held many
banners, signs, and flags demanding the right to vote: "Votes for Women!"
and "Forward into Light!" Many onlookers pushed and shouted at
them. But the world paid attention. It was a new kind of fight—a fight they
would soon win.

INEZ MILHOLLAND

1886–1916

YOUR
VOICE
MATTERS

One young woman who stood out on the day of the 1913 parade was Inez Milholland, a lawyer and workers' rights activist, who led the procession on horseback. When she heard some organizers didn't want African American women to march, she insisted that black students from Howard University be included in the education section.

Inez rode a white horse named Grey Dawn. She wore a crown with a star, which she called the star of hope, and even carried a trumpet to herald a new day. The image of her riding at the front of an army of women inspired many people.

Sadly, Inez died a few years later, still battling for women's right to vote. Her final public words were "Mr. President, how long must women wait for liberty?" This question became the rallying cry for the movement. Inez proved that her voice truly mattered, in life and in death.

Orphaned at sixteen in Holly Springs, Mississippi, Ida B. Wells fought for her place in the world her whole life. When she was only twenty-two years old, a train conductor told Ida to give up her seat because she was sitting in the ladies' coach, which he said was only for white women. Ida had a first-class ticket, so she refused to move. Three men dragged her out. As soon as she got home to Memphis, she sued the railroad. Even though she didn't ultimately win her court fight, her bravery inspired later activists.

Ida became a respected journalist who wrote about her experiences and the violence and injustice faced by African Americans throughout the country. She believed that "the people must know before they can act, and there is no educator to compare with the press." Ida founded the Alpha Suffrage Club of Chicago in 1913 to organize African American women to fight for voting rights. During the 1913 parade in Washington, D.C., she ignored racist objections and marched with the otherwise white Illinois delegation on behalf of the Alpha Suffrage Club. To encourage others, she wrote: "The way to right wrongs is to turn the light of truth upon them."

LUCY
BURNS
1879-1966

PERSISTENCE
is
POWERFUL

Like her good friend Alice Paul, Lucy Burns learned from the suffrage campaign in London that fighting for change requires boldness and persistence. After the 1913 parade's success, she and Alice decided on a new tactic to bring attention to their cause—four years later, they began a silent vigil outside the White House. Protesters carried banners in purple, gold, and white, as well as signs with messages. Some bore Inez Milholland's final words. These women were known as the Silent Sentinels. They stood outside the White House holding signs for five months before police began arresting them. Even then, they did not stop.

In an article in the paper she and Alice published, Lucy urged the sentinels to stay strong and called them an "unconquerable army." Sometimes the women were jailed for months—including Lucy, who was arrested several times and spent the most time in jail—all because they dared to protest.

MARY
CHURCH
TERRELL

1863–1954

STAND
TOGETHER

Mary Church Terrell was a teacher and served on Washington, D.C.'s board of education, the first African American woman to hold such a position. Her fight for suffrage inspired many because, like Sojourner Truth, she challenged the unique discrimination against black women and insisted they be included in the national women's suffrage movement. In 1896, Mary helped found and lead the National Association of Colored Women. She spoke around the country and around the world, praising the "valiant service" of black women who "knock at the bar of justice and ask for an equal chance."

Mary knew it wasn't fair that some white women wanted to exclude women of color from the suffrage movement. She advised the Howard University students of Delta Sigma Theta, a sorority of black women dedicated to public service, and organized them to march in the 1913 parade. Despite a segregated society and having to fight to be included, the Howard University sorority sisters proudly marched together in the education section. In the final push for national women's suffrage, Mary and her daughter Phyllis protested outside the White House as Silent Sentinels. Mary continued to fight against discrimination, knowing that not until *all* women reached their full potential could America reach its.

Finally, in 1919, Congress passed the Nineteenth Amendment, and it was ratified in 1920. It guaranteed women the right to vote—more than seventy years after Elizabeth Cady Stanton helped organize the Seneca Falls Convention. It would be another forty-five years before that right was protected for African American women and men in many southern states. Today, women have far more rights, but the fight for equality and justice continues.

On January 21, 2017, millions of people across the country marched once more so that women's voices could be heard. I remembered the stories of the courageous women whose lives and sacrifices shaped this country— and thought of the march that Alice Paul dreamed up more than one hundred years ago. I stood in front of the crowd of women gathered in Washington, D.C., wearing bright pink hats and called out: "We want to be counted. We want to be heard. We are going to fight for what we believe in, and we are not turning back."

Now it's your turn.

    You are the suffragists of our time. What would you change if you could? Stand up, speak out, and fight for what you believe in. Be bold and be brave. The future is yours to make.

A Quick WALK Through American History

 **Phillis Wheatley (c. 1753–1784)**
Phillis Wheatley, an enslaved woman, achieved international acclaim when she published *Poems on Various Subjects, Religious and Moral* in **1773**. The first African American poet to be published, she was emancipated shortly after the release of her book.

 Abigail Adams (1744–1818)
Just months before the Declaration of Independence was signed in **1776**, Abigail Adams reminded her husband, John, to "remember the ladies" when he and other members of the Continental Congress were crafting a "new code of laws" to govern the country.

 Sacagawea (1788–1812)
This Shoshone woman helped guide the Lewis and Clark Expedition of **1804–1806**, which was commissioned by President Jefferson to explore and begin mapping the vast territory acquired in the Louisiana Purchase.

 Mary Elizabeth Bowser (1839–?)
Like Harriet Tubman, Mary Elizabeth Bowser was once enslaved but became an important spy during the Civil War (**1861–1865**). She infiltrated the house of Confederate president Jefferson Davis as a servant and provided valuable intelligence to the Union.

 Marie Louise Bottineau Baldwin (1863–1952)
A member of the Turtle Mountain Band of Chippewa Indians, Marie Louise Bottineau Baldwin was the first woman of color to graduate from the Washington College of Law. She was appointed to the Bureau of Indian Affairs in **1904** and was also treasurer of the Society of American Indians.

 Jeannette Rankin (1880–1973)
The first woman elected to Congress was a suffragist from Montana who won her first term in **1916** and supported the formation of the congressional Committee on Woman Suffrage. Many years later, in 1940, she won a second term.

 Frances Perkins (1880–1965)
The first female member of a U.S. cabinet, Frances Perkins was secretary of labor from **1933** to 1945. She was active in the labor movement and instrumental in implementing safety regulations to protect workers. She also helped to develop Social Security, an important government program that ensures some financial support for older Americans.

 Marian Anderson (1897–1993)
A distinguished classical singer, Marian Anderson made history when, after being denied a chance to sing at Constitution Hall based on her race, she performed "My Country, 'Tis of Thee" on the steps of the Lincoln Memorial in **1939**, which millions heard on the radio.

 Rosie the Riveter (1943)
When World War II (**1939–1945**) took many men overseas to fight, American women, like my great-grandmother, entered the workforce in droves. A poster featuring a woman called Rosie the Riveter was part of a campaign to increase productivity on the assembly lines, where women helped to make aircraft, armaments, and more for U.S. soldiers. Rosie would become an iconic image, symbolic of women's empowerment.

Wonder Woman (1941)
This female superhero burst into comic books in **1941** and onto the small screen in the 1970s and was the star of a major motion picture in 2017. This character has been an idol of little girls everywhere for generations. (Notice the resemblance to Inez atop Grey Dawn!)

 Linda Brown (1943–2018)
Her family was one of the plaintiffs in the historic *Brown v. Board of Education* case of **1954**, in which the Supreme Court ruled that laws creating separate schools for black and white children were unconstitutional and inherently unequal.

 Dolores Huerta (1930–)
Dolores Huerta is a community organizer and labor leader. Along with Cesar Chavez, she co-founded the United Farm Workers in **1962** and is a voice for the rights of immigrants and women.

 1950s and 1960s
African American women of all ages, including **Dorothy Height, Fannie Lou Hamer, Pauli Murray, Anna Arnold Hedgeman, Myrlie Evers-Williams, Rosa Parks, Diane Nash, Gloria Richardson, Daisy Bates, Prince Lee**, and **Coretta Scott King**, drove the civil rights movement forward toward voting rights and the abolition of Jim Crow laws by organizing boycotts, sit-ins, and Freedom Rides. Their efforts ensured that hundreds of thousands of protesters came to Washington in **1963**, where Martin Luther King Jr. gave his famous "I Have a Dream" speech.

 Shirley Chisholm (1924–2005)
Shirley Chisholm was the first black woman elected to the House of Representatives in **1968**, with the campaign slogan "unbought and unbossed." She ultimately became the first black candidate to run for the presidential nomination of a major party.

 1960s and 1970s
A "second wave" of activism for women's rights expanded the conversation to include protections against workplace discrimination, reproductive rights, and equal opportunities in education and sports. **Bella Abzug, Florynce "Flo" Kennedy, Gloria Steinem, Dorothy Pitman Hughes, Betty Friedan, Audre Lorde, Alice Walker, Mary King, Jo Freeman**, and **Heather Booth** were some of the key voices of this era's feminist movement. In **1972**, Congress finally passed the Equal Rights Amendment, written by Alice Paul in 1923 and revised in 1943, to end gender discrimination under the law, but it has not been ratified by the states.

 Billie Jean King (1943–)
A champion athlete who won numerous tennis tournaments . . . but no contest was more famous than her "Battle of the Sexes" match against Bobby Riggs in **1973**. She is a passionate supporter of women in athletics and a prominent voice in favor of Title IX, the law that mandated equal access to school sports for girls and women.

 Sandra Day O'Connor (1930–)
In **1981**, she became the first woman named to the Supreme Court. Today, for the first time in history, three women serve simultaneously and with distinction on the Supreme Court: **Ruth Bader Ginsburg** (1933–), **Sonia Sotomayor** (1954–), and **Elena Kagan** (1960–).

 Maya Lin (1959–)
When she was an undergraduate student in architecture, Maya Lin submitted a design to the national competition for the Vietnam Veterans Memorial. The contest was "blind," meaning no one knew the identity of the architect. She won, and today the Vietnam Veterans Memorial Wall, which opened in **1982**, is a striking, somber tribute to those who gave their lives in the Vietnam War.

THE RIGHT OF
CITIZENS OF
THE UNITED STATES
TO VOTE SHALL
NOT BE DENIED
OR ABRIDGED by
the UNITED STATES